PRISONER OF THOUGHTS

ARE YOU FEEDING YOUR BRAIN WITH THE RIGHT THOUGHTS?

INDRANI GUHATHAKURATA

This book is dedicated to my father who taught me resilience, not by preaching but by practicing. He is the true epitome of resilience to me.

This book is also dedicated to all those folks who think they are too old to identify their passion and make a difference in their lives.

A quote for my dad:

"Any man can be a father, but it takes someone special to be a dad."- Anne Geddes

Contents

ACKNOWLEDGEMENTS

I would like to express my gratitude to all my mentors, directly or indirectly, whom I came across in these past two years of my awesome journey.

I would like to extend my heartfelt thanks to one of my old friends, who suggested that I read a specific Self-Talk-the book that paved the way for my transformation, and ever since then there's no looking back.

My gratitude to Mr. Giri, for believing in me and for being my source of strength and motivation.

My special thanks to Dr.Subra Mukherjee, for always encouraging me to do my best.

I

INTRODUCTION

"We are what our thoughts have made us, so take care about what you think. -Swami Vivekananda"

Little did I know that every day is a day to shine, our presence is a gift to the world, to leave a sparkle with our own thoughts.

Over the past five decades of my life, if I must single out one of the biggest lessons that life has taught me, it is the realization of the fact- "The mind is the most powerful tool in shaping our lives and we must take care to choose how we think and what we think. We are the product of our thoughts!"

The objective of this book is not merely telling stories from the years gone by, it is about offering practical wisdom through personal accounts. Through this book, I wish to give you a voice and guidance. I understand how difficult it can be when your dreams are put on hold because of someone else's beliefs. I understand how challenging it can be to pursue your dreams when everybody around is doubting you.

The message that awaits inside the book "Prisoner of Thoughts" will provide insights into why certain things- both good and not so good, happen along our path, and how they can help us achieve a better understanding of ourselves, thereby helping us accept ourselves without feeling lost anymore.

Through this book, I want to tell you that it is never too late to find your passion. It is never too late to start. This book aims to break all those belief systems that have been stopping you from living the life you want. It's okay to be a late bloomer.

What Do You Mean By Belief System?

A belief system is a set of principles that interpret our daily life. It is a network of beliefs that we hold about ourselves or things, irrespective of what is right or wrong. Beliefs are like habits that have become ingrained in our minds. They may have started as something you knew to be true, but over time your certainty about them became so strong compared with other possibilities or doubts from outside sources, that it turned into an unthinking habit without leaving any room for doubt. When we become rigid about something, it means that our minds have been convinced of the truth.

A belief system simply put is just having certain preconceived notions towards different things in life such as your family/friends etc., which you carry through every day without questioning them.

It was in the year 2020 when I first got hold of a Self-Talk book, and since then I got fully involved in research about belief systems, how they are formed, and how they impact our lives. And in the process, the lens through which I perceived life became clearer. I got so deeply involved in the process, that I started reading books, interviewing people, and having deep conversations. And with each passing day, my conviction that thoughts can make us or break us kept growing stronger and bolder.

But how do we adopt new belief systems that align with our life goals? How do we shed off the old belief systems that only keep us trapped in vicious circles of self-doubts, shame, procrastination, insecurity, and emotional crisis?

We often adopt belief systems from our surroundings and experiences. Most of it happens subconsciously, but it is possible to adopt positive belief systems that align with our life goals through conscious efforts taken in the right direction. (And this book is all about helping you find that direction)

In order to build a new belief system, you need to lay a strong foundation through daily rituals and good habits. Also one needs to replace the negative self-talk with positive affirmations and shift focus towards 'I CAN' from 'I CANNOT'. This creates consistency which will eventually guide you in the right direction in life. Another vital aspect is to ensure that the whole mindset is geared towards learning 24/7 because knowledge never sleeps.

This book is an attempt to reach out to all the dreamers and help them realize how powerful they can be with just a little shift in their belief system. We must realize that we are unique creations of God and we are capable of doing magnificent things, but the tragedy is that only a few people realize this special power within us. Some have discovered their potential; some are yet to discover their true potential.

This book aims to help people find out their inner strengths and eventually find their purpose in life. This book is about my transformational journey of two years-the two years of my life that brought along a lot of learnings and realizations coupled with peaks and valleys, and I believe this might inspire someone out there, just like how I had been inspired to write this book.

I do not expect a dramatic change in mindset overnight, but if even a single person is benefitted from this book, I will consider my purpose being served. A single person can bring about an enormous change in our lives. The power is within you. If you can take just one good point from this book, I will feel accomplished. It will be my pleasure to help you discover your potential.

I just want you to know this- You are incredible! Yes, You are.

You can live every single day in the best possible manner by asking questions to yourself because the quality of your life depends upon the quality of your questions. If you ask a good question, life will give you a good answer. If you ask a lousy question, life will give you a lousy answer. If you are comparing yourself to another person, remember, you are insulting yourself and your creator too. Remember, you are the best person to answer all your questions.

What gives you satisfaction? What do you wish to do for the rest of your life? What gives you Joy? Only you have the answers to all these questions. It is you who must decide. You are the person who knows what will give you the highest level of satisfaction. You can create your world every single day through your thoughts and your actions.

"Don't drown in a sea of negativity when you can float on the ocean of life. You are meant to be a wonderful, loving expression of life." - Louise Hay

I believe it is my responsibility to share my consistent learnings with my readers because sharing is growing. Let's walk together and experience this amazing ride!

There used to be a time when I ignored myself, to a point that the dreams that were there deep down inside me since my childhood days started fading, and the worst, I was so ignorant that I failed to even understand the injustice I was doing to myself.

I am fortunate that today I understand the power of thoughts. I know the importance of self-talk. And most importantly, I have walked the path.

The Almighty made us for a purpose, to make our life meaningful by giving us the power of dreaming-the power that we all possess. We all have the power to walk that extra mile, but we are not ready to take that single step for our growth. We have the power not only to dream but we have a purpose in life. And once that purpose is identified, one will find every reason to jump out of bed every single morning.

Why waste your life in self-doubt and negativity, when it can be beautifully designed with your belief system? A belief system that can transform you into a remarkable person and you leave a legacy behind. Nothing is impossible when you decide to concentrate on the power you possess by birth. You must just look for it by careful observation.

Childhood Dreams

"Dreams are the seedlings of reality." -Napoleon Hill

We all have dreams but that often remain only a wish unless we define our dream with a time and date and turn it into a GOAL.

We all remember when we were children and had the world at our fingertips. We could imagine anything, and go on an adventure without any limits because there weren't limitations in our minds yet! As a child, our dreams were endless because they were not limited by any knowledge or belief systems. We believed in magic. We believed in bedtime stories. But then...we grow up and somehow that sense of wonder gets dulled over time- like something you can never bring back no matter how hard you try.

However, a close look at ourselves will tell us that the child-like curiosity is still alive within us, only that it has lost its purpose and has become dormant. It is said that children's dreams are magnificent. But as we grow up, we mature and fail to recognize how magnificent we are.

I was no different. I too had a lot of dreams with endless curiosity. I used to share my dreams with my mother, who with a big smile on her face and a gentle nod always assured me, that I was capable of fulfilling all my dreams. Unaware of the fact of what lay ahead, together we had many fun-filled moments and created some of the most beautiful memories of my life in the process.

I remember eagerly waiting for the Durga Puja festival when I would receive a beautiful dress, stitched by my mother, and how I would dance around with that new dress waiting impatiently for the occasion to arrive. Crying for the lost tooth, playing with friends, visiting my grandparents' place, and occasionally visiting the South Indian Restaurant with my parents are some of the fond memories of my childhood.

Undoubtedly, childhood is the best season of life when our dreams have no boundaries. We jump, we fly, and we soar as if some wings have been implanted in us.

We had a small garden area with colourful flowers blooming all around just like my colourful dreams. But something strange happened one day and now I know how symbolic it was. One fateful evening, our garden caught fire and soon the flower buds stopped blooming, and within a few days, my mom was diagnosed with cancer. And soon she left us forever, only to be in my heart for the rest of my life. All my dreams were crushed just like those burnt flower buds. Suddenly, the child in me was dead and all dreams and desires fell apart like a sandcastle being wiped away by a huge wave.

I was blessed to have a wonderful father who sacrificed his whole life for my happiness. He did his best to never make me feel the absence of my mother. Life caught its pace and before I could even realize it, I became an adult-an adult with accumulated belief systems from the surroundings, and an adult who had forgotten how to dream. There was no one to teach me to believe in my dreams.

I was told by the outside world that life was all about scoring good marks and getting a handsome 9 to 5 job. Or rather I would say I was conditioned with this belief system.

Soon, I became a prisoner of my thoughts.

Time went on and I became a prisoner of my thought process. I was left with no option but to follow in the footsteps of those around me. I became the result of my surroundings. I was only aware of dreams with closed eyes, not dreams with open eyes because of my fixed mindset.

Life had been a rollercoaster ride. As I struggled with my conditioned mind and self-doubts, I also developed resilience. I learned how to be resilient from my father, and how to survive in times of adversity. He has been the best example of resilience as he had the power to bounce back from setbacks. I have never found him complaining about anything. He is always in a gratitude mode. I learned this gratitude practice from him which was one of his core values. He seemed to be always smiling but deep down I knew there was always this pain of losing his partner so early in his life. If somebody asked me the definition of a Superhero, my father was the perfect example. Both of us were good badminton players and people used to watch us play with great surprise. He is 82 now and is healthy and active. He is my ultimate source of inspiration, you can say, my bounce-back factor.

The transformation from being a 'Prisoner of Thoughts' to becoming the person I am today; there's so much life has taught me. And with this book, I wish to walk you through all that learnings and experiences and tell you how powerful you are.

You have that magic in you.

Before we begin to dive deep into the book, take your time and reflect upon the answer to the questions below:

1. Mention your two most favourite childhood dreams that faded away as you matured.

2. What is the reason that we get detached from our dreams as we grow up?

3. Do you still have child-like curiosity?

4. Are you afraid to chase your dreams?

You might need one day, one minute, or one year to come up with these answers, but believe me, they are worth every bit of time investment that you will make to arrive at the answers.

II

POWER OF DREAMING

"Abundance is our birthright. Prosperity is our birthright. Yet oftentimes trapped in the clutches of beliefs, self-doubts, and negative self-talk, we fail to realize the power within us, the power of dreaming, the power of becoming Awesome you.- Indrani Guhathakurata"

We all share one thing in common- We all dream!

Irrespective of our age, demographics, background, and social status, we all dream. Or rather I would say, we all dare to dream. This is a special gift we humans are blessed with.

The dream is a powerful thing. It's the fuel that inspires every single day of our lives with new possibilities for growth in all aspects-personality development, career development, and hobbies! And while other living beings only age over time (and their prospects can seem bleaker), humans have an opportunity at evolving too; just look how much change has happened since yesterday: today you might find yourself pursuing something entirely different than last week (or last month, or last year) due to some unexpected inspiration from within-your true voice speaking up for you.

The world is a canvas for your dreams. It's up to you what colour, shape, or size they will be!

The most important thing about having those kinds of thoughts is to never be judging them; just let yourself dream whatever comes into the mind without fearing if it would come true or not. We all have a creative force inside of us, and that power is what drive our dreams. When you dream about something it means your mind has created its own reality- one where anything can happen!

Dreams are essential and play the role of a differentiator in our lives. We all are unique creations of the Almighty, and we have been gifted with the power of dreaming, and the power to make those dreams true in our experience.

The power of imagination is a prized possession, and we should use it to its fullest potential. If you want something done right away-first create the idea in your head, then bring reality into play! That is why it is said, you are the creator of your imagination, create it beautifully. If you want to do something unique, first it should be created in your imagination, then it comes into reality. This is the power of dreaming. We are all born with this amazing power to manifest anything in our life.

But we use it in a negative way by doubting ourselves. We often have great ideas, but fear of failure prevents us from going ahead with our ideas. Fear of change and fear of others' opinions hold us back from doing great things in our life. Fear of rejection is so strong that we often settle with our present situation thus accepting the existing pattern of our belief system.

But why do people fear rejection?

That's because they take it personally. Period.

We must understand this- Rejection is not personal. In life there will always come rejections and obstacles we have no control over; It is obvious that not everybody is going to like what you are doing, they may reject your opinion about something, however, if you take it personally, you are giving others the power to judge your self-worth. They have not rejected you; they have simply made a choice to reject your idea, and that has nothing to do with your self-worth. They have just expressed their opinion. Besides, everyone has the right to make a choice, the right to reject or accept an idea as much as you do.

When you understand this simple logic, you realize how futile it is to take rejections personally. Instead, you must try to find out the blessings in your rejections because this will push you to bring out the best in yourself. When we get rejected or hit with a snag, it's important that instead of focusing on what went wrong and letting negative thoughts consume us, we should rather focus on the path ahead. Rejections just like approvals are part of life. So, instead of getting disheartened or getting trapped in self-demeaning mode, you should start accepting them and learn from them. The word "rejection" should not be seen as a failure, but as one step closer to success. One step closer to your dreams. When we realize this simple truth, then no one has the power to decide your self-worth, and rejections are just a thing to be embraced as much as approval.

We are all imperfect but to find beauty in imperfection is the source of happiness.- Japanese Proverb

Our dreams help us to believe in ourselves, they give us the motivation to make changes in our lives and take daily action. They also give us a sense of accomplishment. Dreams are about pushing yourself to bring out the best in you because you know there is a lot more inside you if you are willing to put that pressure in the right direction. Great changes only happen when you dream about something to give meaning to your life. When people dream, they may end up in something more satisfying and develop certain skills that can make someone feel accomplished as well! This is the reason dreams have a lot of positive impacts on people's lives. For instance, imagine you never thought it was possible for you to pen down your experiences and learnings in the form of a book. But then one day you dream of doing it. You set goals. And then eventually you write, publish, and become an author. Imagine what a feeling that would be. Yes! Indeed, that is the power of dreaming. Power of self-talk. Power of positive thoughts. It gives you a triumphant feeling and an increased level of well-being.

Dreaming requires nothing, hence, it is the first step in achieving something in life. Dreams offer opportunities and hope for all because without hope people feel empty and unfulfilled from inside with their current situation or direction they are on. It is not always about winning or losing, it is about what you are becoming in the process of pursuing your dreams. It is about how strongly you believe in your dreams and yourself.

Here comes the role of self-belief. The set of beliefs that you have about yourself can make or break you. You are the pilot of your life. You can change the direction of your life by consciously making simple choices. Your choices can either open or shut innumerable doors. Life offers you enormous opportunities every single day. It is for us to decide and make choices that are best aligned with our capabilities. When we stop believing in ourselves, our focus is only on surviving, not on thriving. Humans normally tend to focus only on the things that have not worked for them and fail to see the abundance that they have in life. This is mainly because of the years of accumulated beliefs and subconscious and conscious conditioning of the mindset that we have been subjected to.

I was no different. I was like any other normal human being, imprisoned by my own thoughts. Until lately, little did I know about this powerful gift that I had, 'The Power to dream and the ability to make them come true'. I didn't realize that I too had something within me to inspire others. However, I am fortunate that through a series of events, situations, and experiences, I realized this truth- "If I can dream, I can achieve it too." I realized that dreams are required to shape our lives. It is there in all of us, a vision deep inside us that helps us in stretching our minds without any restriction. These dreams bring out our creativity and help us choose a path from the many options we have in our lives. It helps to realize our potential and act accordingly. All we need to free ourselves from all those negative self-talk and believe in ourselves.

But How Do We Train Our Minds To Believe In Ourselves?

1. *Well, for this we first need to change our attitude.*

We need to conquer our limiting beliefs. Every day, we need to remind ourselves that the potential for our lives is unlimited. I know initially, it all sounds like a fairy tale, something that is far away from reality. I have been there myself, and I know how hard it can be to believe in yourself, especially when your memories backed up with the ever-judging society create new obstacles for you every single day. I know how hard it can be to believe in yourself and your dreams, especially when everyone around you is judging your dreams, and rejecting your ideas. Yes, at times it feels like a never-ending storm.

But today I can strongly say that there's one thing stronger than all those obstacles: Yourself!

Always believe in yourself no matter what the situation is because by not believing in yourself, you become your own biggest enemy.

When you believe in yourself no matter what comes your way - you're telling yourself a new story about who you want to become.

2. *Next, you need to be very particular about your daily routine.*

Your daily routine will create your future. Creating healthy habits will increase your creativity and help in unlocking the power within you. Your habits determine your future. Making healthy choices now can have a profound impact on how you live, think, and feel in the coming days and years!

3. Feed your mind with constructive thoughts

Feeding your mind with constructive thoughts will help you focus on the right things in the right direction at the right time. We all have those moments of self-doubt; however, we should use the power within ourselves to overcome these feelings. Self-doubt is merely a state of mind that we can overcome by being open-minded. An open mind does not restrict anything, it does not get bogged down by trivial judgements. An open mind allows you to believe in your own abilities and focus on the abundance that you have.

4. Power of Self-talk

The voice in your head is an important part of how you interact with the world and yourself. The thing about self-talk is It can be just as powerful for negative thoughts too! If there are negative beliefs deep down telling us that we're not good enough or smart enough, and imagine what might happen if they come out into full view. Yes, it is scary. And hence, I want to emphasize that self-talk is a very powerful tool needed to help our mind develop that strong sense of confidence and self-belief. This is discussed in the coming chapters in detail.

5. Willingness to change

"I do not fix problems. I fix my thinking. Then problems fix themselves."- Louise Hay

Now the question is, are you willing to change? The most important thing is finding something that you are passionate about enough to overcome challenges. It is about developing clarity as to what changes you need to make for your desired dream. It means being ready to involve yourself in a series of actions that will lead to your desired outcome. Some may accept a problem as a problem while others may find a solution to that problem. At times we feel our capabilities are limited because of our fixed mindset, but we are not. We always have the power inside us to direct our minds to search for problem-solving solutions, but we fail to realize the power of our brain as a powerful tool to change our way of thinking.

We have always been putting our dreams aside for years, has it worked for you? Then why not follow your dreams and see what happens. The results might surprise you. It does not matter how long you have been in self-doubt or negativity; the point is whether you are willing to change from this moment or not. We cannot change the weather, the people, the situation, the future, the animals or the past. But we can control our thinking to react to different situations in our life. Everything starts with us, the way we think, talk, react, and behave. We must make sure that we learn from our mistakes daily. Even if it has been a bad day, we must think of appreciating at least the little effort that we have made to improve our day. Believing that even if something was not the way we wanted it to be, the following day will give a much better result, gives us a good feeling. By thinking positively, we start attracting positivity into our lives. We cannot change the situation, but we can change our attitude towards that situation.

As part of the research work for this book, I interviewed a few women in the age group of 30 to 60 years, to know about their belief systems, dreams, and various aspects of life.

And the results were pleasantly surprising. Irrespective of their age, they all had some dreams. Dreams that they had been holding close to their hearts, but because of one or the other reason, most of them could not pursue them. And a closer analysis revealed that mostly, it was their own fear of rejection, self-doubts, and years of mental conditioning that they had mostly never dared to use the amazing power they had- *'The power to dream and make true.'*

Another common observation in most of the women was, that while they felt a strong need for a transformation, they were not able to leave their comfort zone and take the plunge. Most of them weren't aware of their own capabilities. In fact, their self-doubt was so strong that they were not ready to accept the fact that how magnificent they are. They believed their capabilities were predestined and cannot be changed or improved. In nutshell, they had a fixed mindset that closed all the doors of opportunities.

On the other hand, there were a few women, who had some interest in learning a new skill and hadn't given up on their dreams. They were open to unlearning the conditioning they had been subjected to. In a nutshell, these women had a growth mindset.

It is unfortunate that a lot of people underestimate the power of thoughts and self-talk and the power within and feel suffocated about life and keep blaming their luck for the same. If someone is successful, they would give the credit to luck. And if they fail, they will again blame it on luck.

Success (and failures) are not associated with luck.

A lot of people feel okay with their suffocated life because they feel success is associated with the lucky ones but this is not true.

What Is Success?

One day, a young lady asked me, "what is the definition of success?"

I believe it is one of the most challenging questions to answer. For ages, the word success has been misunderstood by people. The majority of people think success is achieved by people with special resources. This traditional story does not work anymore. People have become aware of day-to-day success.

Success can mean different things to different people, but if I had to choose one word that accurately describes my definition it's- "WHO I HAVE BECOME TODAY?" If I am a better person or better version today, compared to yesterday, in thought process, in to-do-list, in attitude, in action, then yes, this is success for me. I believe the journey of life is a continuing process and success for me is not a destination. It is the experience I feel each day when I see that I am evolving. It is the joy I experience when I know I am growing in life. Success to me does not mean achieving something very big. Rather, it is contained in those day-to-day power habits, which will eventually help me accomplish bigger things in life.

Success like History, Physics, Maths, Chemistry, and Geography, is a subject too, that has a certain set of principles to follow. One must go through the process to attain the level of success. Success also means opening yourself to challenges that enable you to grow and develop, mentally, professionally, and spiritually. Success is a personal thing. There is nothing more meaningful than following a life of development and betterment. It is through improving ourselves that we get the most out of life.

The good news is that there is never an end to the journey of self-improvement for a dreamer. Dreaming is an uplifting feeling and it gives us a purpose in life. Without our dreams, we are nothing because our success in life and the big & small daily wins, everything start with a dream.

Your determination, your courage, and your passion will ultimately lead you towards the desired success.

Remember, you are never too late to find your passion.

"When we are no longer able to change a situation, we are challenged to change ourselves."-Viktor Frankl

So, are you ready to challenge yourself and take control of your life into your own hands? If yes, take your time and answer these questions to yourself. Be as clear and specific as possible.

1. Do you feel that something is missing in your life, that could have given a different meaning to your life? What is that and why do you feel so?

2. Do you feel fear of rejection and others' opinions has stopped you from chasing your dreams?

3. Do you feel that it's too late to find your passion?

4. Do you feel that there's a need to change your present habits, for a better life ahead?

These questions are designed to make you feel uncomfortable at first, but then gradually you will be able to see through everything clearly. The answers to these questions will help you gain a better understanding of yourself.

III

REALIZATION FOR TRANSFORMATION

> ***"There is only one thing that makes a dream impossible to achieve: the fear of failure.***
> ***— Paulo Coelho, The Alchemist"***

It is said, that the most defining realizations of your life happen at the most unexpected times and often in ways you have never imagined. It is nowhere close to one of those moments when the protagonist would have some divine voice speaking to him/her and then suddenly a transformation happens (what we are used to watching in movies). In reality, it just happens, but then years later when you think about it, you realize the importance of that moment.

It was yet another mundane Monday morning of my life. I was getting ready for the office while rushing through my breakfast, and searching for a file when I quickly caught a glimpse of myself in the mirror. I don't remember exactly what I saw, but it felt like I haven't looked at myself eye-to-eye in years. Of course, I did look in the mirror every day but that was more like yet another chore. I haven't noticed those slight wrinkles under my eyes. That day I felt I was looking at a person whom I had been ignoring for years. The person in the mirror appeared a stranger-A stranger I wanted to know more about, a stranger I desperately wished to befriend.

I sat on the small table kept in front of the dressing mirror and before I realized it, it was 10.30 a.m. I realized that I had been sitting there for more than 2 hours. And what did I do in those two hours? I probably have no answer to that yet. I just sat there looking at myself in the mirror (something so unusual for a person who would spend less than 5 minutes/day in front of the mirror).

That morning suddenly, I felt the hurriedness in me was missing. I wasn't worried about getting late to the office. I wasn't anxious, or worried like I usually would do. Instead, I felt a sense of calmness settling in me. It felt like I had befriended the stranger I saw in the mirror. Now we were one.

That fine morning, I realized that the 9-5 job where I had been working for decades was not for me. It's time to make the change from a "limited" person to the "unlimited" dreamer inside of me! That morning I realized what I had been missing in my life. It felt like there were always other people taking priority over what truly mattered most to me: exploring new opportunities, living an adventurous lifestyle full of growth, and most importantly-chasing my dreams.

I realized the kind of fixed mindset I had developed over the years. I felt somewhere stuck with my unlimited dreams. I realized that all these years of my adulthood, I had been drifting far away from my dreams.

As I said, it was nowhere close to what we watch in movies, like you realize something and your life changes dramatically.

In reality, realization is just the first step. I understood how important my dreams were to me. But I had no idea where to go from here. While the destination seemed to be clear, the path was yet to be defined.

Not knowing what to do, and where to start, I started looking for opportunities to learn something different, some new skill. But as I mentioned earlier too, it's never easy to break that pattern of beliefs and situations. But at the same time, deep within I knew, that this time I would give everything it takes to pursue my dreams. I was nearing my half-century then (two years back).

Few of my well-wishers even told me "Indrani, are you crazy looking for opportunities at this age?"

But I was confident. I had my new friend beside me (the person in the mirror).

"Yes, my dear, I am crazy because life without craziness is not a great life," would be my typical reply with a little smile on my face.

At times self-doubt would grip me and I questioned myself, "what am I searching for?"

"Am I capable of making a difference in my life?"

But the next moment, I would focus my attention to address the bigger concerns. I wanted to find out my purpose in life, I wanted to give meaning to my life, but did not know how to do it. I wanted to define my life, I was searching for something that would give me the highest level of joy and satisfaction, but something was holding me back.

It took me a while to finally figure out what was holding back all of the progress that had been made. It turned out there was only one reason: The belief system that I had been accumulating over the past 5 decades. My own negative belief system worked against me as well as against my well-being. That is the point I realized I needed some kind of transformation to rediscover myself. Thus began the journey of self-discovery, which is infused with great learning experiences.

Beginning Of A New Journey

I got introduced to a new opportunity just before the 2020 lockdown, which later on I realized was a great learning platform. I had only some information about it but no proper knowledge. We had to undergo a lot of training and meetings. We were also asked to go through books, which was the last thing I would do. But I started following all the daily rituals that I was asked to follow and gradually I realized that something much bigger was unfolding in my life.

I started enjoying being a part of the community and without even realizing it, soon I began to motivate people to achieve their goals in life. In fact, I felt motivated myself, motivating people. Reading books started becoming my top priority and at present, they are my most trustworthy friends and the most important tools for my personal growth. I had found my passion in reading, and writing small motivational content.

But the worst was yet to come. On one hand, there was my strong motivation to go ahead and make a difference in my life and that of others, while on the other hand the equally strong obstacles in various forms. It was obvious that I would not sail smoothly. There were some strong winds to resist me from going ahead. Not everybody was going to support me or clap for me. I had to be my own cheerleader and keep moving. But, with each passing day and with every new obstacle, my passion grew stronger, and I became more resilient.

I learned this the hard way- 'You must be your biggest fan!'

On several occasions, I felt confused and thought of giving up. But deep down, I knew that was not what I wanted. Despite all the negativities around me, I continued with my passion. I just did not want to be a spectator in my life, I wanted to be a player, and winning or losing did not matter to me at all. I knew that I could guide people with my knowledge and that gave me the courage to move ahead in confidence. At this juncture, my only support was my father. He has always been my ultimate source of inspiration. He is the person who taught me how to survive through the adversities of life. It was during one of those days, that a friend of mine suggested I go through a self-talk book. I read that book several times and came to the understanding that there has to be a way out to define my own life with my own thoughts.

I just could not be the **PRISONER OF MY OWN LIMITED THOUGHTS.**

I must break through this self-imposed PRISON to evolve as a new person. I decided that I must change, not for the sake of change but for growth; as change is the only constant in life. If you do not adapt to changes, you will soon find yourself lagging behind. When you change the direction of your life for a better reason, it gives you the happiness you deserve in life.

You are everything that is, your thoughts, your life, your dreams come true. You are everything you choose to be. You are as unlimited as the endless Universe."

- Shad Helmstetter, Author- What to say when you talk to yourself!

From the self-talk book, I realized how self-talk can improve our life. The author says that the human mind is extremely powerful and if tuned in the right direction, it can create magic. It can turn your dreams into reality, no matter what your present situation is. But most of the time, things don't work that way, right? Because most of the time our life is decided by others. Out of concern, our near and dear ones make us stay in our comfort zone, and we also take it for granted, and the story of our life is mostly written by others. The author continues to say, "Layer upon layer of our brain has been programmed by negative affirmations" and we never tried to change it because we were unaware of the fact that it could be changed by positive affirmations.

This self-talk book opened up a whole new world to me. One thing was becoming clear to me that I was the person of my own thoughts and that I needed to change that thought process if I wanted to make a difference in my life.

No one has ever encouraged us to think in a different way, to develop thinking skills or entrepreneurship skills. Hence, it automatically got conditioned in that traditional way without even realizing the fact that we can be our best versions. God does not want us to be the best, but to do our best because we are capable of doing something unique in our life. But are we doing justice to the power within us with the right thoughts and actions?

I would like to mention one of my favourite quotes by Todd Henry, "Don't go to your grave with your best work inside you. Choose to die empty". It is our challenge to realize the goodness inside us to build a meaningful life. By your firmness, you can break the self-imposed wall that stands between you and your dreams. Give yourself that mindset to break through the wall to get you where you want to be. Our past has been controlled by others but now we can change it by choosing our thoughts by choosing the way we talk to ourselves. Remember, you are always given a choice as to how you want to spend your time. Even the busiest people on earth find time to do something they choose to do.

If I want to make a difference, my internal dialogue (self-talk) should be, "I choose to spend time in a way that will give me the highest level of satisfaction and help me create my best version." If your mind is tuned with the right self-talk, it will help you go in the right direction. The greatest challenge that we face in our life is to manage and direct our thoughts and emotions but all of these can be managed by the right self-talk. When we acquaint ourselves with positive self-talk, it goes deep inside our subconscious mind and gives direction to act in a positive way. When we give ourselves the right challenge with positive self-talk, our mind will work to make things happen for us, just like certain things (negative self-talk) in the past had worked against us to hold us back from realizing our superpower.

Still wondering, how self-talk can impact our lives? Well, these examples will help you understand better.

Not every day is a good day and we often say, "It was such a miserable day or a problematic day." Now, this statement will always make your subconscious mind search for a difficult pattern whereas if we say, "Today was okay and I learned so many things," our mind will register things in a different way.

Another example of how self-talk can hold us back from learning a new skill.

At times, our self-talk directly works against us when we say, "I want to learn a new skill but it involves a lot of challenges, I don't think I can go for it." This kind of negative self-talk will direct your brain not to learn any new skill. Your mind will register this pattern and you won't be able to learn any new skills.

Similarly, if you keep on telling yourself, "I am the last person to go for book reading, you will never be able to read any book, however with the opposite self-talk, "Book reading is fun, I enjoy reading and writing," your interest will grow with each passing day.

So be careful about what you say to yourself because words are powerful. It may work for you or against you. You are the person responsible for programming your mind. You should have the courage to break through the pattern in your life that no longer serves you.

Transformation is not easy, because you cannot remain positive for 24 hours a day. But you need to adopt some powerful habits for personal growth to develop a strong mindset. This will make your transformation journey enjoyable and productive with small wins.

Let's discuss some of the power habits that can yield maximum growth in your transformation journey.

1. Reading and Writing are powerful habits to improve yourself every day. It improves concentration and focus. It broadens your horizon and allows your mind to be open to new possibilities. Reading and writing also improve your critical thinking skills.

2. Listeningto others makes you a better person. Sometimes our belief system can limit our opportunities. So, developing a habit of being open-minded and listening to others' perspectives allows the mind to unlearn old beliefs and become a better person.

3. Getting more organized is an effective tool for growth. You need to take care of your daily, weekly, and monthly rituals to stop procrastination. Now, why do we procrastinate? Self-doubt leads us to procrastinate. We want better results but we aren't ready to engage ourselves with self-discipline and consistency. The Comfort zone is a great threat to progress because there is no shortcut to becoming your best version. There will be no perfect situation, time, and place to start anything new. You just need to have the attitude, "I will start right now." "I will do it" is okay but "I have done it" gives you a great feeling. Even twenty minutes of learning every day from books will make you an amazing, awesome person.

4. Health is wealth. We all know that a fit body and a healthy lifestyle can improve your productivity as well as your creativity. Whatever we wish to do in life, no matter how big or small our dreams are, we must have this one thing by our side, for everything to happen- i.e., **GOOD HEALTH**. Making healthy food choices, and sticking to a healthy lifestyle will have a direct positive effect on our potential.

5. Consistency and discipline are a must for every individual to grow in life. You have to be consistent to walk that extra mile to get what you truly deserve. That extra can make you extraordinary.

6. You must develop the habit to **say NO** to things that prevent you from being positive.

7. Maintaining some distance from the gadget is a must, instead, enjoy what is around.

8. Think beyond limits and you may end up with a lot more ideas for your interest areas.

9. If your task is a long one, **short breaks** are required to recharge your energy batteries. Some days can be taken off just for fun. **Recreation is as important as work.**

10. Getting connected with a **community or an organization** will help you in getting more connections for your work.

11. Life is full of distractions, so you need to **prioritize** your work, otherwise, you may slow down.

12. Any kind of win, big or small, starts with **believing in yourself** that you can do it. If at times, you feel a lack of motivation, look at the mirror and you will find that the person in the mirror is your best friend.

Make self-talk with positive affirmation your daily habit and you will see transformations happening in your life like never before.

Self-talk is powerful, way more powerful than we imagine. Hence, I wish you to answer the following questions to yourself and assess your current state. These questions will help you gain a better understanding of where you stand and identify what are the things you need to do, to leverage the power of thoughts through positive self-talk.

1. Have you ever felt the need to transform from your present self to a new one?
2. Have you ever realized that your self-talk is working against you?
3. Mention at least three negative self-talk statements that you feel need to be changed immediately with positive self-talk.
4. Do you spend at least 20 minutes reading a book? If not, start now.
5. Do you manage your time effectively?
6. Do you feel too distracted by the outer world?
7. Are you conscious about your health?
8. Do you often procrastinate?

9. Do you listen to others with empathy?

After you have answered the above questions, write down a set of 10 affirmations aligned to your dreams.

IV

WHAT IS THE MINDSET?

> ***"If you have a strong mind and plant in it a firm resolve, you can change your destiny."***
> ***-Paramahansa Yogananda***

A Mindset is a series of self-perceptions or beliefs people hold about themselves. These determine their behavior, outlook, and mental attitude towards everything. Developing a positive mindset is not easy. It takes time and effort to change your perspective, but the rewards are worth every bit of it. It is not as easy as flipping the switch ON. It takes days, months, and years to change your mindset. But it is possible. Yes, it is all about believing in yourself.

Today, when I look back at my younger self, I realize how much I have been ignoring myself because of my fixed mindset. The fountain inside me was trying to come out and spread its beauty, but my programmed brain suppressed it. And this is not just about me. It is about everyone. We must take this first step to recognize our inner potential by changing our mindset.

Carol Dweck, professor of psychology at Stanford University, is best known for her work on mindset. Dweck has extensively studied the differences between a growth mindset and a fixed mindset. According to Dweck, individuals with a growth mindset believe that their abilities can be developed, while those with a fixed mindset view intelligence and abilities as static traits. This distinction has important implications in all areas of life from personal to professional, health to finance, and relationships to wellbeing.

What is the difference between a "fixed" mindset and a "growth" mindset?

The fixed mindset is all about being perfect. Believing that you are either good or bad at something with no room for improvement. The growth mindset is all about being open to learning new things and evolving as a person.

The fixed mindset believes that talent is the key to achievement. But a growth mindset believes that passing through a difficult phase is yet another great learning opportunity for them. People with a fixed mindset often feel inadequate about themselves and often compare themselves with others. They are often scared to step out of their comfort zone and avoid stretching their limits. Their focus is always on finding reasons for not growing in life. They often play the victim card (mostly unknowingly).

Growth mindset, on the other hand, often accepts their weaknesses and works on them to improve their limitations. Fixed mindset people often see things as predestined but the growth mindset believes that with the right kind of action things can be changed.

Fixed mindset often gives up easily stating, "What is the use of continuing with no result?" On the other hand, a growth mindset will develop resilience on their journey towards a goal. Fixed mindset is often scared of failures and avoids challenges whereas the growth mindset considers failures as a stepping stone towards success because they have the power to control every situation by being resilient.

New tasks will always involve challenges, and this is the reason, a fixed mindset always avoids them by sticking to their comfort zone. But the growth mindset will always search for new skills as they feel these are the tools for self-improvement. Growth mindset will always spend some time in self-reflection to measure their gradual progress whereas a fixed mindset will take themselves for granted. People with a growth mindset are not discouraged, rather they celebrate failures, rejections, and challenges and often flourish in times of adversity. Sticking to things even when things aren't going well is the indication of a growth mindset. In the growth pattern, it is all about stretching yourself like a rubber band to learn a new skill and develop yourself, priority is given to learning, not success or failure. For the growth mindset, the focus is only on learning and improving.

It is seen that a growth mindset has a greater resilience. In simple words, a fixed mindset avoids challenges and growth embraces the challenges. Growth mindsets learn from criticism accepting them as feedback, motivation, informative input, and a wake-up call.

Fixed mindset will avoid criticism and say, "I have nothing else to offer to anyone." Growth mindset will say, "How can I offer something to anyone with my best ability?"

You may hear people with a growth mindset saying things like:

It's never too late to learn.
This failure is a learning experience.
Criticism helps me become better.
I can always improve something.
My results don't define me.

As adults, we face a lot of challenges. We juggle work, family, and social obligations and hence, it's easy to get bogged down by stress and let our mindset slip into negativity and self-doubt. But it's ever late to change that! You can start fostering a growth mindset in yourself and reap the benefits of happiness, success, and productivity right now by changing the narrative you have been feeding your mind with.

Is it going to be easy to make the shift? Of course not.

Is it impossible to change your mindset after a certain age? Of course not.

Expecting the process of changing our belief system and our mindset to be quick and easy is an unfair expectation. We have been subconsciously feeding our minds with all kinds of junk food and unhealthy food for so many years now. Hence, making the shift is going to be challenging and it will happen gradually. But the key here is to be aware and take that first step right now and then continue on that path until a growth mindset becomes your natural way of being.

Why Is A Positive Mindset Important?

Mindset is not only important to change your direction in life for a better reason but it is also a powerful tool to discover your true potential.

A strong and positive mindset is important in developing healthy self-esteem. It affects our beliefs, attitudes, and feelings about ourselves. Developing a positive mindset means making positive thinking a habit, constantly searching for that silver lining, and making the best out of any situation you find yourself in, searching for a solution to every problem. With a positive mindset, you can achieve emotional balance, which helps the brain to execute functions properly. A positive mindset means that you have an expectation that things will turn out well and you will succeed. A positive mindset radiates positive energy and gives you a sense of satisfaction. With a positive mindset, you can find happiness within yourself instead of looking for external factors. Did you know that we are born with happiness within us? It requires a positive mindset to unlock that happiness.

At times you will find things are not as bad as they seem to be, just a little shift in your mindset is what we require to see the light. This is the kind of mindset we require to make a difference in our lives. We don't have to like everything we face in our lives, but with a positive mindset, we can go for the better. A positive mindset will always be curious about learning and questioning like, "How is it done or what is it all about or why is it so?"

You all must have noticed how children are curious about everything, they are always eager to learn and ask a lot of questions in their mind. They are the true examples of a growth mindset. Also, you must have noticed how they struggle with their writing skill in the beginning, and later on, with practice and effort, they develop the art of writing neatly. Initially, we all struggle with a new skill but with repeated efforts, we can master it with a positive mindset. People with a positive mindset are always looking for the next possible step to improve themselves. They are unstoppable in their journey to success.

How To Develop A Positive Mindset?

1. Try to focus on the right things by eliminating the unnecessary ones.

We will have good as well as bad times but accepting them as a part of our lives will build our inner strength and make us resilient. You may have negativity around you but knowing to avoid them will improve your focus in the right direction. A positive mindset is when you don't allow negativity to consume your inner goodness.

2. Gratitude practice is a must to develop a positive mindset.

Developing an attitude of gratitude helps us to appreciate every little good thing happening every single day. We must be thankful for being part of the Universe. If you are wondering how to connect with God, then starting your day with a gratitude note is the best way of praying to God. The feeling of gratitude improves sleep and increases feelings of happiness and a positive mood. It also reduces stress and improves resilience. Gratitude practice is essential for enjoying your life. Researchers have shown that people who practice gratitude show significantly higher levels of happiness and well-being. Just two consecutive weeks of daily gratitude practice has lasting positive effects on one's level of optimism. It is a huge booster for physical and mental health. Gratitude means choosing to focus your time and attention on the things you appreciate. Gratitude opens our hearts by connecting us to the wonderful ordinary things that we otherwise take for granted. In times of hardships and emotional turmoil, practicing gratitude acts as a psychological booster, one that does not allow us to give up. Most importantly, gratitude controls our thoughts. We can uplift our thoughts by practicing gratitude every day. It is a powerful tool to enjoy life even when we are going through challenging times. Keeping a gratitude journal and counting your blessings every day will help you to focus on the positive things in your life.

3. Spending time with positive people- This will never allow you to drown in a sea of negativity. Environment plays a crucial role in shaping our life. Hence you need to be careful about whom you spend your time with. Don't allow negative people to feed on your energy. Spending time with positive people will make your life cheerful and you will pay more attention to good things rather than focusing on negative things. A positive environment will make you walk away from things that aren't worth your time. You will find that being with a positive individual will give you a better sense of well-being. Why does this happen? The effect of a person's happiness influences the other person's mood and thus everyone radiates happiness and there is no place for negativity in that circle. Thinking positively has a positive effect on health, as well as reduces stress while improving your overall wellbeing. Just being around positive people makes you more lively, motivated, and inspired. It is said that when like-minded people come together miracles are bound to happen.

4. Choose your words carefully- Often we are very particular when talking with others. We choose our words wisely and make sure we sound kind and appreciative to the listener. But on the contrary, we hardly think when we speak to ourselves. You can develop a positive mindset by choosing to speak to yourself in a constructive manner. It may seem difficult initially as we are more prone to negativity, but with awareness and practice, it is possible. Positive self-talk is your internal narrative that will lead to improved self-esteem and confidence in your own abilities. Not only this, but positive self-talk also improves your mental health and gives you greater life satisfaction. Research has shown that positive self-talk can improve self-confidence in students. Mostly we have the habit of saying things like, "I can't do this, this is not my cup of tea, I am not good enough for anything, I always mess up things or I can't learn any new skill" and all these work against us. If we replace all of these with positive self-talk like, "I will try this, I can learn it with practice, I will do my best, or I will not give up whatever may be the situation", we will find our life filled with positive energy. It's not about winning or failing; it's about improving your narrative about yourself. It's not that your positive self-talk will immediately resonate with your thinking but at least we can say positive things for ourselves instead of focusing on our weaknesses. You never know what you will become by believing in yourself.

5. Adopt powerful habits- Identify your negative areas and replace them with powerful positive habits that will nurture your mind for developing creative skills. You will find yourself emerging as a new person with thinking skills and innovative ideas. When you gain a better understanding of self, you will know what motivates you, and what inspires you and hence you will be your biggest guide. It will be easier for you to identify your interest areas.

6. Start your day on a positive note- This is an essential habit for developing a positive mindset. It's true not everything is going to be positive but we all have a choice to choose wisely. Planning your day and how it can be best utilized will give you a sense of satisfaction for the whole day. You can start your day by being grateful for at least 3 things every day. You can think of going through something that will keep you inspired for the whole day.

Why Is It So Difficult to Change our Mindset In The Later Stages Of Life?

The example of an oak tree will make it clear. Oak trees develop a very deep rooting system and they are connected to all other oak trees, maybe for miles around. All are interconnected and it is hard to change because of the deeply connected roots. But for a baby oak tree, it is much easier to go deep down and take the root system out. Likewise, as we get older, we get more and more conditioned with our existing mindset or belief system and we tend to remain the same. But if we are treated with the right kind of mindset from an early age, we will have the growth mindset to go ahead in life.

Your mindset is everything as it plays a significant role in determining your life's outcome. The bottom line is you must unlearn to learn something new.

Ask yourself the following questions; probably the answers could open up a whole new world of opportunities for growth and success.

1. Which mindset do you feel you belong to?
2. Do you feel you are stuck because of your mindset?
3. Do you feel a new mindset can give you new results?
4. Are you thankful for all the things in your life?
5. Are you ready to challenge yourself and develop a mindset that aligns with your dreams?

V

HOW DOES THE BRAIN WORK?

"Our thoughts are powerful. They can liberate us as well as imprison us. It is up to us to make the right choice- Indrani Guhathakurata"

One of the biggest confusions of all times- Is the mind and brain the same? Often, we hear people using these terms interchangeably. Well, the mind is associated with the brain. The brain is a physical thing and the mind is mental. Mind refers to a person's thought process. Whatever you are thinking in your mind, that information is processed in the brain, so the mind uses the brain, and the brain responds to the mind. Our brain is the most powerful personal computer and that can give you remarkable results if you allow your brain to feed on the right thoughts. When humans do something for too long, it becomes a part of their natural behaviour and creates a pattern in the brain. There's this human psychology that does not like any change and that is the prime reason we procrastinate when starting something new. Whenever there is a challenge, the brain feels uncomfortable and starts creating excuses as to why we shouldn't be doing that. These excuses are nothing but the brain's way of stopping us from going outside the comfort zone. And if these patterns of excuses and procrastination are not nipped in the bud, it can become a dangerous affair, turning us into lifelong prisoners of thoughts and negative beliefs.

This kind of negative self-talk prevents us from taking any action.

We have seen in the previous chapters, the extent to which self-talk can influence our reality. But now we also know how to reverse that equation. You can replace these negative thoughts with positive ones gradually over a period of time. It might take a week, a month, or a year and when you do it repeatedly, your previous brain patterns gradually change and your brain feels comfortable and that is when your uncomfortable zone becomes your comfort zone because your brain has started accepting the new pattern. It is of course easier said than done, but it is not difficult either. All you need is to give some time to your brain to align with the new pattern. Nothing happens overnight, you need to have patience for something good to happen. Similar is the case when learning a new skill. What seems difficult in the beginning may seem easier with your consistent effort.

When you constantly nurture your brain with the right thoughts, it will be conditioned to produce similar results. It has been found that it is always better to start with a 100-day plan to remove your negative thoughts with constructive ones, after which you will develop new ways of thinking, doing, and communicating. People usually do not like the discomfort of change because our brain already has a comfort pattern, as conditioned since our early age.

Positive or negative thoughts can have several changes in the brain. Positive thoughts help your brain to unleash its creative potential, increase attention span, and improve problem-solving skills. It also promotes overall well-being. When you repeatedly and deliberately feed your brain with good thoughts, it will yield results that can change your perspective towards life. Your brain gets conditioned constantly with the information that you feed into it. If you constantly complain, gossip, find excuses, etc; it will make your life much easier according to your thoughts, regardless of your surroundings. Similarly, if you constantly search for opportunities, abundance, and things to be thankful for, it will make it much easier to reflect on those things around you. It takes a great amount of practice but over time, this is a powerful way to reshape your life.

Why Is It That We Are Always Distracted?

Dandapani has explained this so beautifully. He says, "We are distracted because we practice distraction. We are never taught how to concentrate or practice concentration. If we are never taught something, how can we practice something? He continues to say that if someone says, "My mind is always wandering," this is not true because the mind does not wander, awareness of thoughts wanders. Let's assume our mind is a big area having various parts of sadness, happiness, sweet memories, sad memories, special incidents, great vacations, jealousy, hatred, love, etc; and we have this ball of awareness, which is allowed to travel to various parts of our mind. Suppose we allow our awareness ball to travel to the part of sadness, it will travel to that part of our mind and the next moment, if we allow it to travel to the sweet memories part, it will travel to that part unless and until we allow it to travel to some other part of our mind. This is how we are distracted. From the time we wake up, we have uncountable thoughts and 80% of them are negative. This happens because our awareness ball does not stick to one part and it has a tendency to flow to the negative areas a number of times, this is the reason our brain is prone to negativity and we often question ourselves, "What if this happens or what if that happens?" We must try to avoid WHAT IF and start acting on WHAT NOW.

When we allow our awareness ball to travel to a certain part and stay there for an extended period of time, that is called concentration and with practice, concentration becomes our habit, and we are no more distracted unless we allow ourselves to be distracted. It is not possible for our minds to register each and everything happening around us. If we start registering so many things at a time, we will probably go mad. So, our mind has a different way of registering only those things that we constantly think about, your mind starts showing you more of that. Let me clear this with an example. Let's assume you want to learn a skill, your mind will start collecting more information about the things, which are in alignment with your constant thoughts. You will be directed to your areas of interest, without you being aware of that. You have to be alert to recognize those areas.

That is why your world is unique, my world is unique. Your mind will show you the things that will resonate with your thinking and my mind will show me the things that will resonate with my thinking.

"Mind is everything, whatever you think, you become."- Gautam Buddha.

So, stimulating your brain with good thoughts will release dopamine and serotonin (feel-good hormones) that help you to remain motivated and reduce stress. People often struggle for moments of happiness by depending on external factors whereas the key to happiness is within you. When we face our fears or do something that makes us happy and give joy back in life through positive affirmations or behaviours - it's amazing how much better everything can become! Happiness matters more to your brain than you could even imagine. In fact, a feeling of joy can be so encouraging for your brain that it will drive you towards possibilities that can open a whole new world of possibilities for you.

You already have everything necessary; we just need to tap into that inner well of joy and energy! Do some things which make us smile--even when there are challenges or negativity around them-and see how quickly these moments turn into positivity. This world is a place of abundance and possibilities and one can define his/her life by cultivating a winning mindset by which the brain rewires itself with positivity. Intention, knowledge, and motivation won't work unless you drive your brain to take daily action. Daily actions done over a period of time will give you amazing results because you have trained your brain for daily rituals. It will drive you to perform those baby steps because of the already conditioned mindset. This is the power of your brain, once you change the direction, it will show you more possibilities in that direction.

Nothing happens instantly, you have to give time to your brain to replace your self-imposed limitation with a new belief system, a belief that is going to reshape your life. It is interesting to know that our brain plays tricks on us every day. If you have started something and you feel stuck, the big question then becomes, how do we take care of this situation? At this time, our brain will play tricks searching for our self-imposed limitations, making us feel more stuck. These are like, "Oh, I don't have supportive people around me or I don't have the right time to start or I will not be able to make it, I could never do that, I don't have the right skill or I don't have the resources to go ahead in my life". But if you push yourself to say, "What can I do in a different way to get a better result or let me try something different and see if I can make any difference or I am always open to challenges" will make your brain react in a different way or you can say in a productive way.

There are so many ways that seem to block our ways of being successful. Sometimes we will be looking for possible solutions in the wrong place, even though deep down we know it is not the right place to look at. Now, what do we do? We need to bring the awareness into our minds that whatever is holding us back is temporary, and that we will find out the root of this feeling of being stuck and move forward.

People unconsciously doubt their success even before taking any action for their goal. This is because of the self-imposed limitations. To get something you never had, you have to do something you never did.

Some of the benefits of constantly feeding your brain with positive thoughts are that it improves your mental productivity, improves your thinking ability and you view your surroundings from a different perspective that will help you to radiate more positive thoughts. Once you tune your brain to be aligned with the right thoughts, it will never be derailed even in times of hardships. When you take your brain to a new dimension, it does not ever go back again.

Let me show you how positive thinking can shape your life by mind mapping. It is an excellent way of allowing your brain to flow with creative thoughts and keywords and putting them down on paper. It is called divergent thinking. Mind mapping has the power to generate creative ideas in a free-flowing manner. You can make use of images, ideas, and keywords. It stimulates the imagination and helps to foster creativity. You just allow your brain to flow in different directions just like the branches in a tree. It keeps on growing unless you allow it to stop. That is why it is also known as radiant thinking. Here's an example of a Mind Map of positive thoughts and their benefits in the figure below.

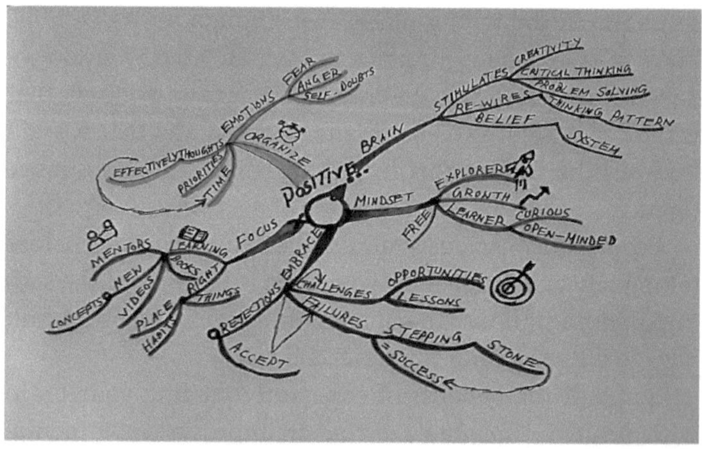

Figure 1- Mind Map on benefits of positive thoughts

Our brain needs to thrive in difficult situations. When your thoughts, beliefs, words, attitudes, and actions are all in harmony, you can create wonders in your life.

The following questions are designed to make you aware of your current state of mind. Answer these questions to yourself. Be honest and descriptive. Allow your thoughts to flow.

1. Do you feel uncomfortable with the thought of adapting to changes in your life?
2. Do you feel you are often distracted?
3. Are you feeding your brain with negative or positive thoughts?
4. Do you have difficulty believing in yourself?
5. Are your thoughts and beliefs and words aligned with each other?
6. Can you commit yourself to three tasks every day?
7. Are you aware of your thought process?

VI

MOTIVATION IN DIFFICULT TIMES

"I think it all comes down to motivation. If you really want to do something, you will work hard for it.—Edmund Hillary"

When it comes to motivation, we often think of some heart-wrenching speeches or videos that get us fired up and we are ready to take on the world. And while these can certainly be helpful in the short term, they often don't lead to lasting change, and we fail to keep up that momentum. So why do we find it so difficult to maintain our motivation? Part of the problem is that we tend to see motivation as something that comes from outside of ourselves. We wait for someone else to inspire us, rather than taking the time to cultivate our own internal motivators. There are several factors that can contribute to why we lack motivation. One reason is that we may not have a clear plan of action. It's one thing to be inspired by someone's story, but if we don't know what specific steps we need to take to achieve our goals, it's easy to become discouraged. Additionally, our environment can play a role in how motivated we feel. If our surroundings are cluttered and chaotic, it can be difficult to stay focused on our goals. Finally, our own mindset can be a major obstacle to staying motivated. If we tell ourselves that we're not good enough or that we'll never reach our goals, it's only natural that we'll start to believe it.

Our environment, especially the people whom we spend our time with also plays a vital role in keeping our motivation level high. If we surround ourselves with people who are inconsistent and have a fixed mindset, it affects us as well. That is why it is said, we are because of our surroundings. When you surround yourself with positive and motivated people, you will also be one of them. It's not that a positive mindset person won't have any problem but they tend to handle it in a different way.

The absence of clarity or purpose in life also often leads to a lack of motivation. Once you have clarity and have identified your passion, you will automatically be directed to set your goals and you will no longer need external stimulation to feel motivated.

Let's consider the game of football. All the players of a team remain highly motivated. Why? Because of the Goal. No Goal, no motivation. Similarly, we need a Goal in our life to keep up the momentum. No external thing can give you motivation, it should come from within. However, there is a difference between a dream and a Goal. A dream does not have a time and date, it is just a wish. While a Goal has a time and date, which helps you to get your desired result within the given time. The goal gives a direction in life to focus on the right things. When you set a Goal, you are setting your priorities and this helps you to focus on the things that align with your Goal. Goal clarifies what matters most in your life. Once you start to improve yourself, you will experience greater self-worth and higher self-esteem. It helps you to sustain motivation even during setbacks and you develop the art of being resilient. It gives you a sense of personal satisfaction. A Goal may seem a big thing, but if you break it up into smaller parts, it becomes easier for you to take action. Small baby steps can help you accomplish your Goal. At first, they might not seem like much but things done over a period of time can give you a compounding effect. This is the reason baby steps are considered to be the stage of progress to achieve your Goal. Self-improvement is the result of these baby steps.

Why are setbacks important and why do we need to train our brains to see failures as an opportunity to grow?

The gap between your starting line and finishing line is your Goal and this gap is loaded with setbacks, failures, rejections, and ignorance, which helps us grow with every action we take. Each and every blow makes you stronger and your brain gets stimulated to search for a problem-solving solution after each setback.

Did it ever cross your mind that failures in life are essential to make you better, not bitter? Life is designed for us to grow and improve. You have to fail in order to grow. You are the only person who has set limitations for yourself by your own thoughts. Don't be a prisoner of thoughts, you need to come out of that self-imposed prison and find out your inner strength. If you have a strong fear of failure, it will obstruct your future endeavours.

You can never know how strong you are until being strong is the only option left for you. It is the unpleasant truth that you will always be tested with negativity, struggles, embarrassment, and disappointments, as long as you are in this world, but all these will liberate your hidden potential.

When Thomas Edison failed nearly 10,000 times to create a lightbulb, instead of giving up, he gained knowledge from each failure that ultimately led him to success. An important lesson gained from failure is to understand what got you wrong. This helps us to develop a deeper understanding of life. The experience of failing completely changes our mindset. It helps in transforming and improving our future selves. Once you realize the importance of failure and how it can make us better in every aspect of life, your mind will be free and you will start celebrating your failures. This is where life teaches us how to sail with the hardships by being resilient. Failures are the best teachers, which we are never taught in school or colleges. If you try to go through life without failing at anything, then you are not really living a great life. Taking risks and falling down, make us into who we are. The reason failure is considered to be negative is that society tends to celebrate only success rather than highlighting the path towards success, as it is filled with setbacks and disappointments. Have you seen a flute? Did you notice the holes in the flute? Why are they so important, can you tell me? Those holes in a flute help to produce various vibrations and sound notes that the player can best achieve while playing the flute. Likewise, our failures are like the holes of the flute, which are required for our growth.

"It is impossible to live without failing at something unless you live so cautiously that you might as well not have lived at all, in which case you have failed by default."
- J.K. Rowling

The Mindset To Adopt When You Are Going Through A Crisis In Life

You must be aware that people who have done remarkably well in life, do things in a different way. We all know that learning a new skill involves a lot of challenges. If someone wants to win a medal at the Olympics, he or she will require to face all the challenges and make all the habit changes irrespective of whether they like it or not, because to them only one thing matter- The Medal. Their brain gets trained with the thoughts of holding a medal in their hands.

Successful people have one thing in common, they are resilient. No matter what life throws at them, they bounce back and keep moving toward their goals. They too are confronted with failures and rejections, but instead of complaining they take invaluable lessons from these chapters of life and keep moving.

We need to understand that certain things take time; hurrying or rushing through the process or feeling bogged down by challenges is not the solution. What is rather needed is patience and resilience. We must understand that inevitable delays are a part of the journey, the process to make us even more capable. Being able to bounce from rejections or any such challenges will take you to greater heights in life.

I had mentioned earlier that our brain also needs some kind of appreciation to perform its functions in a better way. But at times we don't get it the way we had expected it to be. Appreciating oneself is very important as it drives people to do their best. It not only allows you to reflect on the hard things that you have done but can also build your confidence.

If no one is appreciating you, or if no one is telling you, "Hey, you are amazing, or you have done a great job," then you need to say these words to yourself. Change the narrative. Tell yourself, "today was simply awesome" or "I did it anyway".

We are all aware that people usually don't appreciate it. Hence, self-appreciation is very important. It is not easy, but we must reward our efforts at the end of the day by remembering all that we have accomplished so far. It could be a small win, but it needs appreciation. I have experienced it and I cannot tell you how rewarding it can be for you too.

It does not matter how little you did, but you need to praise yourself every day. Whatever you want to hear, just say it to yourself. As I was writing this book, I used to say, "Oh! I created this paragraph this is too good or I really like the title I have created for my book." And after finishing every chapter I used to say, "This book is awesome or a lot of people are going to benefit from this book," and it did wonders for my confidence level. I could have said, "This is not good, I don't like it or how can I write when I have not written before." I was given a choice but I chose to be positive in my brain about my writing. So, you always have a choice in life, you need to choose carefully to get the most out of your life.

It's okay to feel miserable after a setback. This is where you need to choose your mindset whether you chose to see the brighter side of the situation or not. Instead of treating it as a setback, it can be considered a turning point in your journey and make you realize that each day is a new beginning. You need to know that we all make mistakes but learning from those mistakes is what actually counts.

While learning to ride the bicycle, we used to stumble and fall but that was part of the learning process. Likewise, we will occasionally stumble and fall, which is part of our journey. To be a changemaker, you have to do something, which you have not done before.

We often crumble after a setback and start finding excuses or blaming people and situations. But remember if you are blaming people, time, or situation, you are actually hurting yourself. We need both the peaks and the valleys to go ahead in life. The peaks will remind you of your purpose in life and valleys help you to take necessary action for that purpose of your life. It's true that challenges and setbacks slow us down, but they also give us an opportunity to restart and reshape our lives. They make us more resilient. Try changing your perspectives, and you will understand that every setback comes with a set of important life lessons. And all these can only happen when you choose to think in a different way and tune your brain accordingly. Remember that with each setback, you evolve as a new person. Life is not going to be easy; you must get stronger and more capable.

Eckhart Tolle was on the brink of suicide before he became one of the most prominent spiritual teachers in the world. Walt Disney was told he lacked creativity. The list could go on. Setbacks, challenges, and rejections are not the end of life, they are the learning tool for the next step.

"A setback is a setup for a comeback."- Willie Jolley

"It is strange but true, that the most important turning points of life often come at the most unexpected times and in the most unexpected ways."- Napoleon Hill

Sometimes you will feel stagnated in life, you feel as though nothing is working for you. This is the period you need to take a pause and look at your inner self. Think deeply and you will realize that this is not stagnation, but rather a stillness, that has its own meaning to prepare you for a better purpose. This stillness can become your best learning period and transform you forever. Things will happen when they must happen. Reflect on yourself and embrace every season of life. Enjoy the roller-coaster ride called LIFE.

Here are a set of 5 questions for you to reflect upon and take actions that are aligned with your goals.

1. Do you feel directionless in your life?
2. Do you have a burning desire for something?
3. Do you feel a lack of motivation in everything you do
4. Do you have a strong fear of failure and rejection?
5. Do you feel setbacks are the end of everything?

VII

WHY CLARITY IS IMPORTANT IN LIFE?

Clarity in life depends on the clarity of mind. Clarity is important because it helps us to set realistic goals and achieve them. When we have a clear vision of what we want to achieve, we are more likely to take the necessary steps to make it happen. Clarity also allows us to better communicate our needs and desires to others, which can lead to more productive relationships. Additionally, being clear about our personal values and priorities can help us to make better decisions in all areas of life. Finally, clarity can simply make life more enjoyable by reducing stress and worry. When we know what we want and why we want it, we can relax and savour the journey towards our goals. Clarity is important because it leads to greater success, satisfaction, and happiness in life. It gives you a direction in life.

A lot of youngsters are disoriented and looking for a transformation in life. They are confused due to a lack of clarity; they need direction in developing their thinking and entrepreneurship skills. As this is their experimental period, they need to connect with various activities to find out their niche. Once they have the clarity, things will get easier, and they can set their goals accordingly. Confusion will be lesser when the deep-rooted purpose of life is identified. They need to decide what kind of life they want to lead, and what kind of daily activities is needed that will give them the highest level of joy and satisfaction, and meaning in their life. If your mind is cluttered and messy, you won't be able to think clearly. First, you need to remove that mess for your mind to work effectively. Sometimes we tend to run in the wrong direction without knowing what we really want in our life. Clarity is when you are defining your life by your thoughts and actions. When you become responsible for your own life without blaming others for your circumstances, is when you become clear about your purpose.

Mind mapping- a thinking process invented by Tony Buzan is one of the effective ways to find clarity in life. Identify what really matters to you and try doing one thing at a time. Getting quiet for some time every day can remove your internal distractions. We have so many thoughts popping up in our minds and sometimes over-thinking impacts our professional and personal life. You can maintain a diary and write down your goals, thoughts that make you happy and sad, your likes and dislikes, ideas, weakness, and your strength, this may help you to focus on the right things and eliminate unnecessary ones. Just let your brain flow with ideas, will give you more clarity.

We have already discussed the importance of a positive mindset in our life but if we don't have clarity in our brains, we will be directionless in our life. With clarity, you can bring confidence back to your life. When you know the reason why you are doing something, it will get much easier to move forward. Sometimes your brain is messy, and you are not able to make a choice but with a clear mind, you will be able to make good decisions. If your mind is not clear, you will have self-doubts, but with clarity, you will only focus on the right things. Once you are sorted out in your mind, it will be much easier to get things done.

Clarity creates a path to achieving your goals. We all are distracted at one time or the other but with clarity of purpose, you will be at ease in handling distractions in your day-to-day life. You will not be able to perform your best because of your scattered focus and this is due to a lack of clarity.

How I Got Clarity?

Two years back, my mind was full of confusions, not knowing what I was missing. But I knew my job won't give me any direction in life. Honestly speaking, books were the last thing I would spend time with. But it is said that when you wish for something sincerely, it comes to you in unexpected ways and that unexpected way was the network marketing platform. I had absolutely no knowledge about this and with the hope of learning something new, I just grabbed it. Gradually I found, it was a powerful platform for personal growth and I was encouraged to go through books, which was a part of our training system. This is the point; I started reading books and writing small motivational content, which gave me immense happiness. This became a daily ritual for me, and I started listening to motivational speakers as well. I thoroughly enjoyed what I was doing. It was clear to me what I was missing in my life. I was not aware that writing could give you so much clarity in life. I started writing my daily journals. This does not mean that by being clear in mind, you will not have problems in your life, but it is just the other way round. Clarity means you need to be prepared for daily actions, and small steps, which will help you to accomplish bigger things in life. Clarity means being responsible for one's life.

Each of us goes through a confusing period in life and it is very normal to have one. It is during this period; we develop the art of remaining cool by being resilient. Your clarity may not come with a single activity, you need to connect with various activities to find out your superpower. Your superpower means your inner strength. You must know what inspires you, what motivates you. We cannot be the best in everything but we can certainly give our best to something, for which we have been sent by the Almighty. The equation of our life is to utilize our full potential and to make the most out of life. You need to watch for those simple signals around you that you actually love doing or are good at and this could eventually end up being your superpower. At times we are closer to that kind of thing, but we are not able to capture it because of a lack of clarity and we end up in great confusion. Once you realize your niche, you will see yourself progressing rather than lagging. There will be a continuous flow and you will start enjoying your work even if it is loaded with challenges. We should be in search of such tools, which can give clarity in life and one such tool is mind mapping.

Each of us has different ideas about what makes us feel good. Clarity can give a meaning to our lives and make it worth living. When you feel lost or directionless in your life, you know how difficult it is to progress on anything. So, with clarity, you get fulfillment and satisfaction in life.

To get clarity you can try mind mapping by which you will be able to find out what inspires you, what motivates you and you will come up with various ideas. The 'WHAT IFs' should not come in the way of your quest for clarity. Be specific about what you want in life and take necessary actions.

Importance Of Small Wins

When you are clear about your thoughts and take actions accordingly, your everyday progress at first might seem unimportant and trivial, but with consistency, you gradually realize the importance of these series of small wins. They are a boost for our brains and release chemicals that give us a feeling of happiness. It's true small wins do not give you a big change, however, they can help you gain more confidence. It creates a sort of momentum to move forward in the right action. When we start acknowledging our small wins, we are celebrating our clarity of thoughts, and this means appreciating small moments of joy and hope. They infuse us with motivation to keep sailing.

Research by Harvard Professor and Author Teresa Amabile shows that a small win is a small amount of progress. She found that people often felt largely motivated and joyful, when they made even a small step forward to their meaningful work. Recent research shows that small wins can even unleash your creativity. The researchers found that people consistently underestimated the importance of small events in their workdays, and this resulted in loss of momentum. Sometimes people are of the opinion that small actions lead to small consequences, but this is not true. When we have a big goal, it is always advisable to break it into smaller parts to make it more manageable. And the gap from the starting line to the finishing line (the person you want to become) is infused with small wins as you cut through various challenges, and find yourself emerging as a different person. Small wins are ways of measuring your progress every single day.

Here's a list of questions for you to answer and reflect upon. These questions are formulated with the objective to help you, deep-dive, into yourself and do some soul searching.

1. Are you sure about what you want to do with your life?
2. How would you like to define your life?
3. What is it that gives you immense happiness?
4. What are the things that people like about you?
5. Mention any three things that you love doing?
6. Mention any three things that you are good at?
7. Having answered these six questions, you might have some clarity to pick up the right track for yourself.

If you have answered the whole questionnaire from chapters one to seven, then by now you have already gained a good understanding of yourself.

You will know your interest areas and things that need to be improved or developed to get clarity in life. You will also know where you need to focus to become the person you want to be. You will also be aware of your priorities in life.

"Remember, you are an ocean of potential, you just need to dive deep into yourself to find out that pearl inside you." - Indrani Guhathakurata

VIII

ARE YOU READY TO BE THE AWESOME YOU?

I believe you have had an insightful experience walking this transformational journey with me- The journey from understanding the power of dreams, to how a belief is formed. And the process of how with the right inner-self-talk and mindset, one can change the trajectory of his/her life. I am certain that you now understand that you have the power to bring out the best in yourself by choosing your thoughts carefully.

The world is full of abundance and possibilities. No matter what difficulties you are facing, you can choose to focus on the positive and make a difference in the world. It takes courage to take up challenges, but it is always worth it in the end. When you step outside of your comfort zone, you open yourself up to a whole new world of experiences and possibilities. So don't be afraid to take a chance – it just might lead you to amazing things.

And I want you to remember this- *'It's never too late to find out your passion. It does not matter when you start dreaming, it only matters that you dream and take the required action to make those dreams happen."*

No matter what age you are or where you are in life, you can always choose and chase your dreams. Your dreams are a blessing in disguise; Just close your eyes for a moment and visualize the time when your dreams are fulfilled. How do you feel? How amazing a feeling, it is! What an experience and sense of accomplishment it will be!

Yes, it is possible.

Isn't it amazing that we can create our own world by our own thoughts? This is the biggest gift as well as our biggest responsibility, that we can create a direction for our future by our own thoughts. When we choose the right thoughts to take us in the right direction, we give ourselves the greatest gift for which we have been created. We are all born with gifts and talents that we can use to make a positive impact on the world around us and it is never too late to change the direction of our life. By taking the time to assess goals and priorities, one can begin to make choices that will lead towards a path of success and significance. It may not be easy, but it will be worth it when we look back at our life and see that we made a difference.

So don't wait any longer, start today and walk the road to doing something remarkable with your life.

However just learning or just understanding won't help, you must take necessary action, and put the things you learn into practice. You must internalize the learnings and make it a way of life to get the best outcome.

When you have the power to control your thoughts, why not feed your brain with the right thoughts? Why be a

Prisoner of negative thoughts? It isn't that difficult but it's worth trying to improve the quality of your life. Why not use your energy in a way that will give maximum benefit to your life?

With a new mindset and belief system, you can give a new meaning and a new direction to your life. It is not essential that external motivation will be from a close friend or family, it can be from someone unexpected too. Sometimes to get something in life, we need to simply believe and start doing it. You may come across people saying, "Nothing is going to change." But it is for you to decide what thoughts you want to feed your brain with.

At times we look for clarity in the external world while the answers lie deep within us. As a result, we end up in frustration and confusion. It is just like painting a house without cleaning it from the inside. To change the fruit, you must remove the root.

Self-Analysis

1 Did you discover the root of your current self, and do you feel the need to change it for the better?

2. Do you feel the need to become person B from person A?

3. Did you enjoy the transformation journey?

I hope the activity given at the end of each chapter has helped you to gain a deep understanding of yourself. I genuinely wish ALL THE BEST for your AWESOME JOURNEY.

Feel free to contact me at guhaindrani147@gmail.com

About The Author

Indrani Guhathakurata

Indrani Guhathakurata is a motivational content writer, a certified Mind Mapper, and the author of the new book PRISONER OF THOUGHTS.

She is an active member of a non-profit International Foundation, whose vision is to empower communities through Art, Culture, Research, and Innovation. She has also worked as a medical transcriptionist for a few years.

She always had a desire to contribute to society by making a difference in people's lives through her writings. She is a firm believer in the fact that each one of us has the potential to make a difference on this earth if we wish to.

Through her first book, 'PRISONER OF THOUGHTS' she aims to help people realize how magnificent they are. And she does this by sharing her knowledge and experiences that she had gained through her own transformational journey, the journey she fondly calls as -**Becoming the Awesome You.**

Printed by Libri Plureos GmbH in Hamburg,
Germany